A Note to Parents

DK READERS is a compelling program for beginning readers, designed in conjunction with leading literacy experts, including Dr. Linda Gambrell, distinguished Professor of Education at Clemson University. Dr. Gambrell has served as President of the National Reading Conference, the College Reading Association, and the International Reading Association.

Beautiful illustrations and superb full-color photographs combine with engaging, easy-to-read stories to offer a fresh approach to each subject in the series. Each DK READER is guaranteed to capture a child's interest while developing his or her reading skills, general knowledge, and love of reading.

The five levels of DK READERS are aimed at different reading abilities, enabling you to choose the books that are exactly right for your child:

Pre-level 1: Learning to read
Level 1: Beginning to read
Level 2: Beginning to read alone
Level 3: Reading alone
Level 4: Proficient readers

The "normal" age at which a child begins to read can be anywhere from three to eight years old. Adult participation through the lower levels is very helpful for providing encouragement, discussing storylines, and sounding out unfamiliar words.

No matter which level you select, you can be sure that you are helping your child learn to read, then read to learn!

LONDON, NEW YORK, MUNICH,
MELBOURNE, and DELHI

Senior Editor Ros Walford
Senior Art Editor Ann Cannings
Production Editor Kavita Varma
Senior Production Controller Rachel Lloyd
Proofreader Eric Titner
Associate Publisher Nigel Duffield

Reading Consultant
Linda Gambrell

First American Edition, 2012
10 9 8 7 6 5 4 3 2 1
001–186471–Aug/12

Published in the United States by DK Publishing
375 Hudson Street, New York, New York 10014

DK books are available at special discounts when purchased in bulk
for sales promotions, premiums, fund-raising, or educational use.
For details, contact:
DK Publishing Special Markets
375 Hudson Street
New York, New York 10014
SpecialSales@dk.com

A catalog record for this book is available
from the Library of Congress.

ISBN: 978-0-7566-9845-4

Color reproduction by Media Development & Printing Co. Ltd., U.K.
Printed and bound in China by L. Rex Printing Co. Ltd.

The publisher would like to thank the following for their kind
permission to reproduce their photographs:
a=above, b=below/bottom, c=center, l=left, r=right, t=top
Dorling Kindersley: John Hughes / Bedrock studios 29; Natural
History Museum, London 4–32tl (even page numbers), 32br.
Jacket images: *Front:* **Dorling Kindersley:** Peter Minister.

All other images © Dorling Kindersley
For further information see: www.dkimages.com

Discover more at
www.dk.com

DK READERS

BEGINNING
TO READ ALONE
2

Dinosaur
Battles

Written by Michele R. Wells

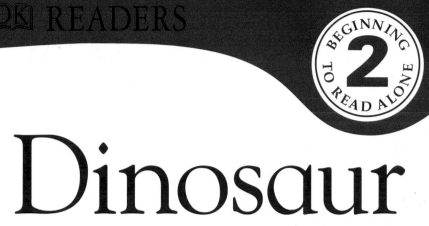

DK Publishing

Introduction

Dinosaurs were reptiles that lived on Earth for more than 160 million years. The last dinosaur died many millions of years before people lived.

The dinosaurs battling in this book might not have lived at the same time or in the same place, but it's fun to imagine them meeting. In a fight over food or shelter, which dinosaur do you think would have won?

| Triassic Period 251–200 million years ago | Jurassic Period 200–145 million years ago |

There is a fact box on each page of this book. The box gives you information about the dinosaur. At the bottom of each page is a battle score. The dinosaur with the highest battle score would probably have won in a fight.

Look at the top corner of each page as you flip through the book quickly. You will see the dinosaur move!

Coelophysis

SEE-low-FYE-sis

This carnivore was a quick, agile hunter. *Coelophysis* used its long neck and sharp teeth to snatch prey from far away.

length **10 feet**
attack **sharp, curved teeth**
defense **strong hind legs**
period **Late Triassic**

battle score

7

Lesothosaurus

li-SUE-too-SORE-us

The plant-eater *Lesothosaurus* was small and speedy. Big eyes on the sides of its head helped it to spot danger from far away.

length 3 feet

attack small teeth

defense speed

period Early Jurassic

battle score

4

Eudimorphodon

YOU-die-MOR-fo-don

Eudimorphodon was a crow-like pterosaur (TEH-roe-sore) that hunted fish in lakes and lagoons. On each wing was a "hand" that could grasp and hold prey.

wingspan 3 feet
attack sharp, fang-like teeth
defense flight
period Late Triassic

battle score

6

Edmontosaurus

ed-MONT-oh-SORE-us

This giant, duck-billed herbivore lived in large herds. Some would watch for danger while the others fed on pine needles, twigs, seeds, and fruit.

length 43 feet
attack more than 1,000 teeth
defense good eyesight
period Late Cretaceous

battle score
3

Tenontosaurus

ten-NON-toe-SORE-us

This large plant-eater walked on four legs. *Tenontosaurus* was heavy and slow, and did not have many defenses. It lived in herds for protection.

length **23 feet**
attack **sharp, bony beak**
defense **clawed feet; long tail**
period **Early Cretaceous**

battle score

1

Deinonychus

dye-NON-ee-cuss

This fearsome hunter was small and lightweight. It attacked using the long claws on its feet. A pack of them could take down a much larger dinosaur.

length **10 feet**
attack **knife-like claws**
defense **speed**
period **Early Cretaceous**

battle score

7

Pachycephalosaurus

PACK-ee-SEFF-ah-low-SORE-us

This omnivore was fast and agile. *Pachycephalosaurus* had a thick, spiky skull. It attacked by ramming head-first into its enemies.

length	16 feet
attack	spiky skull
defense	speed; good eyesight
period	Late Cretaceous

battle score

6

Euoplocephalus

YOU-owe-plo-SEFF-ah-luss

The short, wide body of
Euoplocephalus was covered in
bony spikes and plates. This
plant-eater often grazed alone,
so it needed
armored body
protection.

length 20 feet

attack club-shaped tail

defense body armor

period Late Cretaceous

battle score

5

Plateosaurus

PLATE-ee-oh-SORE-us

With its long neck, this herbivore could reach high into the treetops for leaves. *Plateosaurus* was big and heavy. It walked on its hind legs and used its tail for balance.

length 25 feet
attack powerful thumb claw
defense tough, scaly skin
period Late Triassic

battle score

2

Eoraptor

EE-oh-rap-tor

This fox-sized hunter was one of the earliest dinosaurs. It ran on its toes like a bird. Its teeth were good for feeding on both meat and plants.

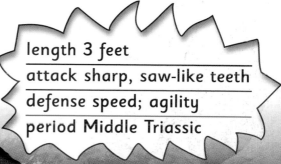

length	3 feet
attack	sharp, saw-like teeth
defense	speed; agility
period	Middle Triassic

battle score

5

Parasaurolophus

PA-ra-SORE-oh-LOAF-uss

Parasaurolophus was an herbivore with a duck-like beak. It had a bright crest on the top of its head. Its loud, trumpeting call could be heard from far away.

length 30 feet
attack long tail
defense good sense of smell
period Late Cretaceous

battle score

3

Triceratops

try-SERRA-tops

This elephant-sized herbivore walked on four legs. It had a bony frill on its neck that helped in defense. *Triceratops* usually traveled in herds.

length 30 feet

attack 4-foot-long horns

defense beak-like snout

period Late Cretaceous

battle score

4

Saltasaurus

SALT-ah-SORE-us

Saltasaurus was covered in bony plates. This herbivore also had a long neck. It could reach plants that other creatures could not.

length 40 feet

attack none

defense body armor

period Late Cretaceous

battle score

2

Sauropelta

SORE-oh-PELT-ah

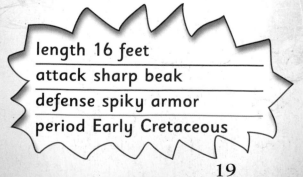

This rhinoceros-like herbivore had thick, short legs. Its heavy, club-shaped tail, neck spikes, and bony armor helped it to defend itself from predators.

length	16 feet
attack	sharp beak
defense	spiky armor
period	Early Cretaceous

battle score

3

19

Stegosaurus

STEG-oh-SORE-uss

This large plant-eater was covered in bony plates. It had a sharp beak, but no teeth. It fought by swinging its spiky tail at its enemies.

length 30 feet
attack spiky tail; bony beak
defense bony plates and spikes
period Late Jurassic

battle score
3

Barosaurus

BAH-roe-SORE-us

Barosaurus was one of the longest dinosaurs that ever lived. It feasted on leaves high up in the trees. It reared back on its hind legs to reach up to 49 feet. That's higher than many buildings!

length **92 feet**

attack **long, whip-like tail**

defense **spines on its back**

period **Late Jurassic**

battle score

4

Pterodactylus

TEH-roe-DACK-till-us

wingspan 12 inches
attack sharp, pointed teeth
defense flight
period Jurassic

This winged creature fed on fish and other marine animals. Its body was covered in hair-like bristles. *Pterodactylus* used the "hands" on its outer wings to climb and to seize prey.

battle score

6

Kentrosaurus

KEN-troh-SORE-uss

This large, slow herbivore had a double row of plates and spines down its back. These served as body armor. Two long spikes jutted sideways from its shoulders.

length **17 feet**

attack **hoof-like claws**

defense **shoulder spikes**

period **Late Jurassic**

battle score **4**

Allosaurus

AL-oh-SORE-us

This fearsome predator had a wide, gaping mouth with knife-like teeth. It ran on its powerful back legs and swiped at enemies with its tough claws. *Allosaurus* hunted large plant-eaters.

length **39 feet**
attack **powerful claws**
defense **huge, swiping tail**
period **Late Jurassic**

battle score
9

Compsognathus

COMP-sog-NAITH-us

This was one of the smallest dinosaurs that ever lived. It ran quickly on the tips of three toes. It fed on lizards and other small animals with its sharp, pointed teeth.

length 3 feet
attack sharp teeth; long tail
defense speed; good eyesight
period Late Jurassic

battle score
6

Nothosaurus

NO-tho-SORE-us

Nothosaurus was a marine reptile that laid its eggs on the shore. It had a neck like a crocodile. It whipped sideways to seize prey.

length	4–13 feet
attack	spiky teeth
defense	camouflaged skin
period	Triassic

battle score
7

Spinosaurus

SPINE-oh-SORE-us

Spinosaurus was one of the largest hunters of all time. It was a fast, agile predator with teeth and jaws like a crocodile. It had a bony crest, or "sail," on its back.

length **60 feet**

attack huge, curved claws

defense stiff-tipped tail

period Late Cretaceous

battle score

8

Citipati

SIH-tee-PAH-tee

Citipati may have been an omnivore. It had a short beak and no teeth. Its body was covered with simple feathers that made it look furry.

length 9 feet

attack tough beak

defense speed; agility

period Late Cretaceous

battle score
5

Giganotosaurus

gig-AN-oh-toe-SORE-us

Giganotosaurus was a fearsome hunter. Its teeth were 8 inches long. That's bigger than a grown-up's hand! Despite its huge size, it had a very small brain.

length	39 feet
attack	knife-like teeth
defense	heavy tail
period	Late Cretaceous

battle score
10

Tyrannosaurus

TIE-ran-oh-SORE-us

Tyrannosaurus was one of the most dangerous carnivores. Its teeth were huge, pointed spikes. It was very quick and agile for its size.

length 39 feet
attack powerful jaws
defense heavy tail
period Late Cretaceous

battle score
10

Therizinosaurus

THERRY-zin-oh-SORE-us

This herbivore's giraffe-like neck could reach up high into trees. The long, sharp claws on its hands made it tough for enemies to get close enough to kill.

length 26–36 feet

attack none

defense 3-foot-long claws

period Late Cretaceous

battle score

4

Glossary

agile
moves easily

armored
protected with
a covering for
defense

attack
threaten
physically

carnivore
an animal that
eats meat

Cretaceous
the last period
of the age of
the dinosaurs

defense
protect oneself

herbivore
an animal that
eats plants

herd
a group of
animals that live
and eat together

Jurassic
the middle period
of the age of
the dinosaurs

omnivore
an animal that
eats both plants
and meat

pack
a group of
animals that
hunt together

period
a portion of time

predator
an animal that
hunts and kills
other animals
for food

prey
an animal that is
killed and eaten
by a predator

pterosaur
a flying reptile

reptile
cold-blooded,
scaly creatures
that usually
lay eggs

scales
small, flattened
plates that cover
the body

serrated
saw-toothed;
jagged like a
steak knife

Triassic
the period when
the dinosaurs
first appeared

wingspan
the distance
between the tips
of a pair of wings